Best Loved Poems

Georges Seurat: *Sunday Afternoon on the Island of La Grande Jatte*, 1884/86.
Helen Birch Bartlett Memorial Collection, courtesy of The Art Institute of Chicago.

BEST LOVED POEMS

OF ALL TIME

Illustrated With Famous Paintings and Drawings.

Selected by Gail Harano Cunningham

♔ Hallmark Crown Editions

Index

June

James Russell Lowell

And what is so rare as a day in June?
Then, if ever, come perfect days;
Then Heaven tries earth if it be in tune,
And over it softly her warm ear lays;
Whether we look, or whether we listen,
We hear life murmur, or see it glisten;
Every clod feels a stir of might,
An instinct within it that reaches and towers,
And, groping blindly above it for light,
Climbs to a soul in grass and flowers;
The flush of life may well be seen
Thrilling back over hills and valleys;
The cowslip startles in meadows green,
The buttercup catches the sun in its chalice,
And there's never a leaf nor a blade too mean
To be some happy creature's palace;
The little bird sits at his door in the sun,
Atilt like a blossom among the leaves,
And lets his illumined being o'errun
With the deluge of summer it receives;
His mate feels the eggs beneath her wings,
And the heart in her dumb breast flutters and sings;
He sings to the wide world and she to her nest—
In the nice ear of Nature, which song is the best?

Now is the high-tide of the year,
And whatever of life hath ebbed away
Comes flooding back with a ripply cheer,
Into every bare inlet and creek and bay;
Now the heart is so full that a drop overfills it,
We are happy now because God wills it;
No matter how barren the past may have been,
'Tis enough for us now that the leaves are green;
We sit in the warm shade and feel right well
How the sap creeps up and the blossoms swell;
We may shut our eyes,
        but we cannot help knowing
That skies are clear and grass is growing;
The breeze comes whispering in our ear,
That dandelions are blossoming near,
That maize has sprouted, that streams are flowing,
That the river is bluer than the sky,
That the robin is plastering his house hard by;
And if the breeze kept the good news back,
For other couriers we should not lack;
We could guess it all by yon heifer's lowing,—
And hark! how clear bold chanticleer,
Warmed with the new wine of the year,
Tells all in his lusty crowing!

Claude Monet: *Banks of the Seine, Vetheuil*, 1880.
Chester Dale Collection, National Gallery of Art, Washington, D.C.

The Passionate Shepherd to His Love

Christopher Marlowe

Come live with me and be my love,
And we will all the pleasures prove
That valleys, groves, and hills, and fields,
Woods or steepy mountain yields.

And we will sit upon the rocks,
Seeing the shepherds feed their flocks
By shallow rivers, to whose falls
Melodious birds sing madrigals.

And I will make thee beds of roses,
And a thousand fragrant posies:
A cap of flowers, and a kirtle,
Embroider'd all with leaves of myrtle.

6

A gown made of the finest wool,
Which from our pretty lambs we'll pull;
Fair lined slippers for the cold,
With buckles of the purest gold.

A belt of straw and ivy buds,
With coral clasps and amber studs:
And if these pleasures may thee move,
Come live with me and be my love.

The shepherd swains shall dance and sing
For thy delight each May morning.
If these delights thy mind may move,
Come live with me and be my love.

Henry Matisse: *Head of a Girl*, from *Poesies de Mallarme*, 1932.
A. Peter Dewey Memorial Gift, courtesy of The Art Institute of Chicago.

7

Auguste Renoir: *Girl with a Watering Can*, 1876.
Chester Dale Collection, National Gallery of Art, Washington, D.C.

Pippa's Song

Robert Browning

The year's at the spring,
And day's at the morn;
The lark's on the wing;
The snail's on the thorn;
Morning's at seven;
The hillside's dew-pearl'd;
God's in His heaven—
All's right with the world!

Pablo Picasso: *The Bee*, from *Buffon*, 1941/42.
Courtesy of The Art Institute of Chicago.

9

The Barefoot Boy

John Greenleaf Whittier

Blessings on thee, little man,
Barefoot boy, with cheek of tan!
With thy turned-up pantaloons,
And thy merry whistled tunes;
With thy red lip, redder still,
Kissed by strawberries on the hill;
With the sunshine on thy face,
Through thy torn brim's jaunty grace,
From my heart I give thee joy,—
I was once a barefoot boy.
Prince thou art,—the grown-up man
Only is republican,
Let the million-dollared ride!
Barefoot, trudging at his side,
Thou hast more than he can buy,
In the reach of ear and eye—
Outward sunshine, inward joy;
Blessings on thee, barefoot boy!
Oh, for boyhood's painless play,
Sleep that wakes in laughing day,
Health that mocks the doctor's rules,
Knowledge never learned of schools,
Of the wild bee's morning chase,

Of the wild flower's time and place,
Flight of fowl and habitude
Of the tenants of the wood;
How the tortoise bears his shell,
How the woodchuck digs his cell,
And the groundmole sinks his well;
How the robin feeds her young,
How the oriole's nest is hung,
Where the whitest lilies blow,
Where the freshest berries grow,
Where the ground-nut trails its vine,
Where the wood-grape's clusters shine,
Of the black wasp's cunning way,—
Mason of his walls of clay,—
And the architectural plans
Of gray-hornet artisans!—
For, eschewing books and tasks,
Nature answers all he asks,
Hand in hand with her he walks,
Face to face with her he talks,
Part and parcel of her joy,—
Blessings on thee, barefoot boy!

By the rude bridge that arched the flood,
Their flag to April's breeze unfurled,
Here once the embattled farmers stood,
And fired the shot heard round the world.

Concord Hymn
Ralph Waldo Emerson

The foe long since in silence slept;
Alike the conqueror silent sleeps;
And Time the ruined bridge has swept
Down the dark stream which seaward creeps.

On this green bank, by this soft stream,
We set today a votive stone;
That memory may their deed redeem,
When, like our sires, our sons are gone.

Spirit, that made those heroes dare
To die, and leave their children free,
Bid Time and Nature gently spare
The shaft we raise to them and thee.

Paul Cezanne: *House of Pere Lacroix*, 1873.
Chester Dale Collection, National Gallery of Art, Washington, D.C.

'He was a friend to man, and lived
in a house by the side of the road.'—Homer

from *The House by the Side of the Road*

Sam Walter Foss

There are hermit souls that live withdrawn
In the peace of their self-content;
There are souls, like stars, that dwell apart,
In a fellowless firmament;
There are pioneer souls that blaze their paths
Where highways never ran;
But let me live by the side of the road
And be a friend to man.

Let me live in a house by the side of the road,
Where the race of men go by—
The men who are good and the men who are bad,
As good and as bad as I.
I would not sit in the scorner's seat,
Or hurl the cynic's ban;
Let me live in a house by the side of the road
And be a friend to man....

Henri Matisse: *Boat* from *Poesies de Mallarme*, 1932.
A. Peter Dewey Memorial Gift, courtesy of The Art Institute of Chicago.

Death Be Not Proud

John Donne

Death be not proud, though some have called thee
Mighty and dreadful, for thou art not so,
For those whom thou thinkest thou dost overthrow
Die not, poor death, nor yet canst thou kill me.
From rest and sleep, which but thy picture be,
Much pleasure, then from thee, much more must flow,
And soonest our best men with thee do go,
Rest of their bones, and soul's delivery.
Thou art slave to Fate, Chance, Kings, and desperate men,
And dost with poison, war, and sickness dwell,
And poppy, or charms, can make us sleep as well,
And better than thy stroke; why swellest thou then?
One short sleep past, we wake eternally,
And death shall be no more; death, thou shalt die.

To the Virgins, to Make Much of Time

Robert Herrick

Gather ye rosebuds while ye may,
Old Time is still a-flying;
And this same flower that smiles today,
Tomorrow will be dying.

The glorious lamp of heaven, the sun,
The higher he's a-getting,
The sooner will his race be run,
And nearer he's to setting.

That age is best which is the first,
When youth and blood are warmer;
But being spent, the worse and worst
Times still succeed the former.

Then be not coy, but use your time,
And while ye may, go marry;
For, having lost but once your prime,
You may forever tarry.

Edgar Degas: *Four Dancers*.
National Gallery of Art, Washington, D.C.

from *Elegy Written in a
Country Churchyard*

Thomas Gray

The curfew tolls the knell of parting day,
The lowing herd winds slowly o'er the lea,
The plowman homeward plods his weary way,
And leaves the world to darkness and to me....

Beneath those rugged elms, that yew-tree's shade,
Where heaves the turf in many a mould'ring heap,
Each in his narrow cell for ever laid,
The rude Forefathers of the hamlet sleep....

For them no more the blazing hearth shall burn,
Or busy housewife ply her evening care:
No children run to lisp their sire's return,
Or climb his knees the envied kiss to share....

Let not Ambition mock their useful toil,
Their homely joys, and destiny obscure;
Nor Grandeur hear with a disdainful smile
The short and simple annals of the poor.

The boast of heraldry, the pomp of pow'r,
And all that beauty, all that wealth e'er gave,
Awaits alike th' inevitable hour:
The paths of glory lead but to the grave....

18

Perhaps in this neglected spot is laid
Some heart once pregnant with celestial fire;
Hands, that the rod of empire might have sway'd,
Or waked to ecstasy the living lyre.

But Knowledge to their eyes her ample page
Rich with the spoils of time did ne'er unroll;
Chill Penury repress'd their noble rage,
And froze the genial current of the soul.

Full many a gem of purest ray serene
The dark unfathom'd caves of ocean bear:
Full many a flower is born to blush unseen,
And waste its sweetness on the desert air....

Far from the madding crowd's ignoble strife
Their sober wishes never learn'd to stray;
Along the cool sequester'd vale of life
They kept the noiseless tenor of their way....

Jean-Baptiste-Camille Corot: *Reading In Under The Trees.*
Courtesy of The Art Institute of Chicago.

Auguste Renoir: *The Wave*, 1879.
The Potter Palmer Collection, courtesy of The Art Institute of Chicago.

Fog
Carl Sandburg

The fog comes
on little cat feet.

It sits looking
over harbor and city
on silent haunches
and then moves on.

I Never Saw a Moor
Emily Dickinson

I never saw a Moor—
I never saw the Sea—
Yet know I how the Heather looks
And what a Billow be.

I never spoke with God
Nor visited in Heaven—
Yet certain am I of the spot
As if the Checks were given—

A Thing of Beauty

John Keats

A thing of beauty is a joy for ever:
Its loveliness increases; it will never
Pass into nothingness; but still will keep
A bower quiet for us, and a sleep
Full of sweet dreams, and health, and quiet breathing.
Therefore, on every morrow, are we wreathing
A flowery band to bind us to the earth,
Spite of despondence, of the inhuman dearth
Of noble natures, of the gloomy days,
Of all the unhealthy and o'er-darkened ways
Made for our searching: yes, in spite of all,
Some shape of beauty moves away the pall
From our dark spirits. Such the sun, the moon,
Trees old and young, sprouting a shady boon
For simple sheep; and such are daffodils
With the green world they live in; and clear rills
That for themselves a cooling covert make
'Gainst the hot season; the mid-forest brake,
Rich with a sprinkling of fair musk-rose blooms:
And such too is the grandeur of the dooms
We have imagined for the mighty dead;
All lovely tales that we have heard or read:

An endless fountain of immortal drink,
Pouring unto us from the heaven's brink.
Nor do we merely feel these essences
For one short hour; no, even as the trees
That whisper round a temple become soon
Dear as the temple's self, so does the moon,
The passion poesy, glories infinite,
Haunt us till they become a cheering light
Unto our souls and bound to us so fast,
That, whether there be shine, or gloom o'ercast,
They always must be with us, or we die.

Pablo Picasso: *The Butterfly*, 1941/42.
Courtesy of The Art Institute of Chicago.

Claude Monet: *Iris By The Pond*, 1919/25.
Courtesy of The Art Institute of Chicago.

Patterns

Amy Lowell

I walk down the garden paths,
And all the daffodils
Are blowing, and the bright blue squills.
I walk down the patterned garden paths
In my stiff, brocaded gown.
With my powdered hair and jewelled fan,
I too am a rare
Pattern. As I wander down
The garden paths,
My dress is richly figured,
And the train
Makes a pink and silver stain
On the gravel, and the thrift
Of the borders.
Just a plate of current fashion,
Tripping by in high-heeled, ribboned shoes.
Not a softness anywhere about me,
Only whalebone and brocade.
And I sink on a seat in the shade
Of a lime tree. For my passion
Wars against the stiff brocade.
The daffodils and squills
Flutter in the breeze
As they please.
And I weep;
For the lime tree is in blossom
And one small flower has dropped upon my bosom.

And the plashing of waterdrops
In the marble fountain
Comes down the garden paths.
The dripping never stops.
Underneath my stiffened gown
Is the softness of a woman bathing in a marble basin,
A basin in the midst of hedges grown
So thick, she cannot see her lover hiding,
But she guesses he is near,
And the sliding of the water
Seems the stroking of a dear
Hand upon her.
What is Summer in a fine brocaded gown!
I should like to see it lying in a heap upon the ground.
All the pink and silver crumpled up on the ground.

I would be the pink and silver as I ran along the paths,
And he would stumble after,
Bewildered by my laughter.
I should see the sun flashing from his sword-hilt and the
      buckles on his shoes.
I would choose
To lead him in a maze along the patterned paths,
A bright and laughing maze for my heavy-booted lover.
Till he caught me in the shade,
And the buttons of his waistcoat bruised my body as he
      clasped me,
Arching, melting, unafraid.
With the shadows of the leaves and the sundrops,
And the plopping of the waterdrops,
All about us in the open afternoon—
I am very like to swoon
With the weight of this brocade,
For the sun sifts through the shade.

Underneath the fallen blossom
In my bosom,
Is a letter I have hid.
It was brought to me this morning by a rider from the Duke.
"Madam, we regret to inform you that Lord Hartwell
Died in action Thursday se'nnight."
As I read it in the white, morning sunlight,

26

Raoul Dufy: *Fountain at Venice*
Courtesy of The Art Institute of Chicago.

The letters squirmed like snakes.
"Any answer, Madam," said my footman.
"No," I told him.
"See that the messenger takes some refreshment.
No, no answer."
And I walked into the garden,
Up and down the patterned paths,
In my stiff, correct brocade.
The blue and yellow flowers stood up proudly in the sun,
Each one.
I stood upright too,
Held rigid to the pattern
By the stiffness of my gown.
Up and down I walked,
Up and down.

In a month he would have been my husband.
In a month, here, underneath this lime,
We would have broke the pattern;
He for me, and I for him,
He as Colonel, I as Lady,
On this shady seat.
He had a whim
That sunlight carried blessing.
And I answered, "It shall be as you have said."
Now he is dead.

In Summer and in Winter I shall walk
Up and down
The patterned garden paths
In my stiff, brocaded gown.
The squills and daffodils
Will give place to pillared roses, and to asters, and to snow.
I shall go
Up and down,
In my gown.
Gorgeously arrayed,
Boned and stayed.
And the softness of my body will be guarded from embrace
By each button, hook, and lace.
For the man who should loose me is dead,
Fighting with the Duke in Flanders,
In a pattern called a war.
Christ! What are patterns for?

Auguste Renoir: *On the Terrace,* 1881.
Mr. and Mrs. Lewis L. Coburn Memorial Collection, courtesy of The Art Institute of Chicago.

Grow Old Along With Me

Robert Browning

Grow old along with me!
The best is yet to be,
The last of life, for which the first was made:
Our times are in his hand
Who saith, "A whole I planned,
Youth shows but half; trust God:
see all, nor be afraid!"

The sea is calm to-night.
The tide is full, the moon lies fair
Upon the straits;—on the French coast the light
Gleams and is gone; the cliffs of England stand,
Glimmering and vast, out in the tranquil bay.
Come to the window, sweet is the night-air!
Only, from the long line of spray
Where the sea meets the moon-blanched land,
Listen! you hear the grating roar
Of pebbles which the waves draw back, and fling,
At their return, up the high strand,
Begin, and cease, and then again begin,
With tremulous cadence slow, and bring
The eternal note of sadness in.

Sophocles long ago
Heard it on the Aegean, and it brought
Into his mind the turbid ebb and flow
Of human misery; we
Find also in the sound a thought,
Hearing it by this distant northern sea.

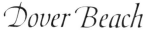

Dover Beach

Matthew Arnold

The sea of faith
Was once, too, at the full, the round earth's shore
Lay like the folds of a bright girdle furled.
But now I only hear
Its melancholy, long, withdrawing roar,
Retreating, to the breath
Of the night-wind, down the vast edges drear
And naked shingles of the world.

Ah, love, let us be true
To one another! for the world, which seems
To lie before us like a land of dreams,
So various, so beautiful, so new,
Hath really neither joy, nor love, nor light,
Nor certitude, nor peace, nor help for pain;
And we are here as on a darkling plain
Swept with confused alarms
        of struggle and flight,
Where ignorant armies clash by night.

The World Is Too Much With Us

William Wordsworth

The World is too much with us; late and soon,
Getting and spending, we lay waste our powers;
Little we see in Nature that is ours;
We have given our hearts away, a sordid boon!
The sea that bares her bosom to the moon;
The winds that will be howling at all hours,
And are up-gathered now like sleeping flowers;
For this, for everything, we are out of tune;
It moves us not.—Great God! I'd rather be
A Pagan suckled in a creed outworn,
So might I, standing on this pleasant lea,
Have glimpses that would make me less forlorn;
Have sight of Proteus rising from the sea,
Or hear old Triton blow his wreathed horn.

Henri Matisse: *Still Life: Apples on Pink Tablecloth.*
Chester Dale Collection, National Gallery of Art, Washington, D.C.

The Village Blacksmith

Henry Wadsworth Longfellow

Under a spreading chestnut-tree
The village smithy stands;
The smith, a mighty man is he,
With large and sinewy hands;
And the muscles of his brawny arms
Are strong as iron bands.

His hair is crisp, and black, and long,
His face is like the tan;
His brow is wet with honest sweat,
He earns whate'er he can,
And looks the whole world in the face,
For he owes not any man.

Week in, week out, from morn till night,
You can hear his bellows blow;
You can hear him swing his heavy sledge
With measured beat and slow,
Like a sexton ringing the village bell,
When the evening sun is low.

And children coming home from school
Look in at the open door;
They love to see the flaming forge,
And hear the bellows roar,
And catch the burning sparks that fly
Like chaff from a threshing-floor.

He goes on Sunday to the church,
And sits among his boys;
He hears the parson pray and preach,
He hears his daughter's voice,
Singing in the village choir,
And it makes his heart rejoice.

It sounds to him like her mother's voice,
Singing in Paradise!
He needs must think of her once more,
How in the grave she lies;
And with his hard, rough hand he wipes
A tear out of his eyes.

Toiling,—rejoicing,—sorrowing,
Onward through life he goes;
Each morning sees some task begin,
Each evening sees it close;
Something attempted, something done,
Has earned a night's repose.

Thanks, thanks to thee, my worthy friend,
For the lesson thou hast taught!
Thus at the flaming forge of life
Our fortunes must be wrought;
Thus on its sounding anvil shaped
Each burning deed and thought!

Auguste Renoir: *Madame Henriot*, 1876.
Gift of the Adele R. Levy Fund, Inc., National Gallery of Art, Washington, D.C.

To Celia

Ben Jonson

Drink to me only with thine eyes,
    And I will pledge with mine;
Or leave a kiss but in the cup,
    And I'll not look for wine.
The thirst that from the soul doth rise
    Doth ask a drink divine;
But might I of Jove's nectar sup,
    I would not change for thine.

I sent thee late a rosy wreath,
    Not so much honoring thee
As giving it a hope that there
    It could not withered be:
But thou thereon didst only breathe
    And sent'st it back to me;
Since when it grows, and smells, I swear,
    Not of itself, but thee!

Non Sum Qualis Eram Bonae Sub Regno Cynarae

Ernest Dowson

Last night, ah, yesternight, betwixt her lips and mine
There fell thy shadow, Cynara! Thy breath was shed
Upon my soul between the kisses and the wine;
And I was desolate and sick of an old passion—
Yea, I was desolate and bowed my head.
I have been faithful to thee, Cynara!—in my fashion.

All night upon mine heart I felt her warm heart beat,
Night-long within mine arms in love and sleep she lay;
Surely the kisses of her bright red mouth were sweet;
But I was desolate and sick of an old passion,
When I woke and found the dawn was gray:
I have been faithful to thee, Cynara!—in my fashion.

I have forgot much, Cynara! Gone with the wind,
Flung roses, roses riotously with the throng,
Dancing, to put thy pale, lost lilies out of mind;
But I was desolate and sick of an old passion—
Yea, all the time, because the dance was long:
I have been faithful to thee, Cynara!—in my fashion.

I cried for madder music and for stronger wine,
But when the feast is finished and the lamps expire,
Then falls thy shadow, Cynara! The night is thine;
And I am desolate and sick of an old passion,
Yea, hungry for the lips of my desire:
I have been faithful to thee, Cynara!—in my fashion.

O Captain! My Captain!

Walt Whitman

O Captain! my Captain! our fearful trip is done;
The ship has weather'd every rack,
  the prize we sought is won;
The port is near, the bells I hear,
  the people all exulting,
While follow eyes the steady keel,
  the vessel grim and daring:
  But O heart! heart! heart!
  O the bleeding drops of red,
  Where on the deck my Captain lies,
  Fallen cold and dead.

O Captain! my Captain! rise up and hear the bells;
Rise up—for you the flag is flung—
  for you the bugle trills;
For you bouquets and ribbon'd wreaths—
  for you the shores a-crowding;
For you they call, the swaying mass,
  their eager faces turning:
  Here Captain! dear father!
  This arm beneath your head;
  It is some dream that on the deck
  You've fallen cold and dead.

My Captain does not answer,
  his lips are pale and still;
My father does not feel my arm,
  he has no pulse or will;
The ship is anchor'd safe and sound,
  its voyage closed and done;
From fearful trip the victor ship
  comes in with object won:
  Exult, O shores, and ring, O bells!
  But I, with mournful tread,
  Walk the deck my Captain lies,
  Fallen cold and dead.

When I Consider How My Light Is Spent

John Milton

When I consider how my light is spent
Ere half my days in this dark world and wide,
And that one talent which is death to hide
Lodged with me useless, though my soul more bent
To serve therewith my Maker, and present
My true account, lest he returning chide,
"Doth God exact day-labor, light denied?"
I fondly ask. But Patience, to prevent
That murmur, soon replies, "God doth not need
Either man's work or his own gifts. Who best
Bear his mild yoke, they serve him best. His state
Is kingly: thousands at his bidding speed,
And post o'er land and ocean without rest;
They also serve who only stand and wait."

Camille Pissarro: *Place du Havre, Paris*, 1893.
Gift of Mrs. Leigh B. Block, courtesy of The Art Institute of Chicago.

The Man He Killed

Thomas Hardy

"Had he and I but met
By some old ancient inn,
We should have sat us down to wet
Right many a nipperkin!

"But ranged as infantry,
And staring face to face,
I shot at him as he at me,
And killed him in his place.

"I shot him dead because—
Because he was my foe,
Just so—my foe of course he was;
That's clear enough; although

"He thought he'd 'list, perhaps,
Off-hand like—just as I—
Was out of work—had sold his traps—
No other reason why.

"Yes; quaint and curious war is!
You shoot a fellow down
You'd treat if met where any bar is,
Or help to half-a-crown."

42

Pablo Picasso: *Combat for Andromeda* from *Ovid's Metamorphoses.*
Courtesy of The Art Institute of Chicago.

Tiger! Tiger! burning bright,
In the forests of the night:
What immortal hand or eye
Could frame thy fearful symmetry?

The Tiger

William Blake

In what distant deeps or skies
Burnt the fire of thine eyes?
On what wings dare he aspire?
What the hand dare seize the fire?

And what shoulder, and what art,
Could twist the sinews of thy heart?
And when thy heart began to beat,
What dread hand? and what dread feet?

What the hammer? what the chain?
In what furnace was thy brain?
What the anvil? what dread grasp
Dare its deadly terrors clasp?

When the stars threw down their spears
And watered heaven with their tears:
Did he smile his work to see?
Did he who made the Lamb make thee?

Tiger! Tiger! burning bright,
In the forests of the night:
What immortal hand or eye,
Dare frame thy fearful symmetry?

A Red, Red Rose

Robert Burns

O, my luve is like a red, red rose,
That's newly sprung in June:
O, my luve is like the melodie
That's sweetly played in tune.

As fair art thou, my bonnie lass,
So deep in luve am I;
And I will luve thee still, my dear,
Till a' the seas gang dry.

Till a' the seas gang dry, my dear,
And the rocks melt wi' the sun;
And I will luve thee still, my dear,
While the sands o' life shall run.

And fare thee well, my only luve!
And fare thee well a while!
And I will come again, my luve,
Tho' it were ten thousand mile!

Paul Cezanne: *Vase of Flowers*, 1876.
Chester Dale Collection, National Gallery of Art, Washington, D.C.

Sea Fever

John Masefield

I must go down to the seas again,
    to the lonely sea and the sky,
And all I ask is a tall ship
    and a star to steer her by;
And the wheel's kick and the wind's song
    and the white sail's shaking,
And a grey mist on the sea's face,
    and a grey dawn breaking.

I must go down to the seas again,
    for the call of the running tide
Is a wild call and a clear call
    that may not be denied;
And all I ask is a windy day
    with the white clouds flying,
And the flung spray and the blown spume,
    and the sea-gulls crying.

I must go down to the seas again,
    to the vagrant gypsy life,
To the gull's way and the whale's way,
    where the wind's like a whetted knife;
And all I ask is a merry yarn
    from a laughing fellow-rover,
And quiet sleep and sweet dream
    when the long trick's over.

Eugene Boudin: *Marine.*
Gift of Mr. and Mrs. W. Eisendrath, courtesy of The Art Institute of Chicago.

Auguste Renoir: *Lady at the Piano*, 1875.
Mr. and Mrs. Martin A. Ryerson Collection, courtesy of The Art Institute of Chicago.

How Do I Love Thee?

Elizabeth Barrett Browning

How do I love thee? Let me count the ways.
I love thee to the depth and breadth and height
My soul can reach, when feeling out of sight
For the ends of Being and ideal Grace.
I love thee to the level of every day's
Most quiet need, by sun and candle-light.
I love thee freely, as men strive for Right;
I love thee purely, as they turn from Praise.
I love thee with the passion put to use
In my old griefs, and with my childhood's faith.
I love thee with a love I seemed to lose
With my lost saints,—I love thee with the breath,
Smiles, tears, of all my life!—and, if God choose,
I shall but love thee better after death.

Jenny Kiss'd Me

Leigh Hunt

Jenny kiss'd me when we met,
    Jumping from the chair she sat in;
Time, you thief, who love to get
    Sweets into your list, put that in!
Say I'm weary, say I'm sad,
    Say that health
    and wealth have miss'd me,
Say I'm growing old, but add,
    Jenny kiss'd me.

Pierre Bonnard: Etching from *Vollard St. Monique.*
Gift of Joseph R. Shapiro, courtesy of The Art Institute of Chicago.

She Walks in Beauty

George Gordon, Lord Byron

She walks in beauty, like the night
Of cloudless climes and starry skies;
And all that's best of dark and bright
Meet in her aspect and her eyes:
Thus mellowed to that tender light
Which heaven to gaudy day denies.

One shade the more, one ray the less,
Had half impaired the nameless grace
Which waves in every raven tress,
Or softly lightens o'er her face;
Where thoughts serenely sweet express
How pure, how dear, their dwelling-place.

And on that cheek, and o'er that brow,
So soft, so calm, yet eloquent,
The smiles that win, the tints that glow,
But tell of days in goodness spent,
A mind at peace with all below,
A heart whose love is innocent!

Wild Spirit, which art moving everywhere;
Destroyer and preserver; hear, O, hear!

Make me thy lyre, even as the forest is:
What if my leaves are falling like its own!
The tumult of thy mighty harmonies

from *Ode to the West Wind*

Percy Bysshe Shelley

Will take from both a deep, autumnal tone,
Sweet though in sadness. Be thou, Spirit fierce,
My spirit! Be thou me, impetuous one!

Drive my dead thoughts over the universe
Like withered leaves to quicken a new birth!
And, by the incantation of this verse,

Scatter, as from an unextinguished hearth
Ashes and sparks, my words among mankind!
Be through my lips to unawakened earth

The trumpet of a prophecy! O, wind,
If Winter comes, can Spring be far behind?

52

Vincent Van Gogh: *Sunny Midi, Arles*, 1888.
Mr. and Mrs. Lewis L. Coburn Memorial Collection, courtesy of The Art Institute of Chicago.

Outwitted

Edwin Markham

He drew a circle that shut me out—
Heretic, rebel, a thing to flout.
But Love and I had the wit to win:
We drew a circle that took him in!

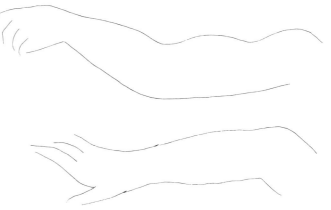

Pablo Picasso: *Two Heads* from *Ovid's Metamorphoses*.
Courtesy of The Art Institute of Chicago.

54

The Chambered Nautilus

Oliver Wendel Holmes

This is the ship of pearl which, poets feign,
        Sails the unshadowed main,—
        The venturous bark that flings
On the sweet summer wind its purpled wings
In gulfs enchanted, where the Siren sings,
        And coral reefs lie bare,
Where the cold sea-maids rise
        to sun their streaming hair.

Its webs of living gauze no more unfurl;
        Wrecked is the ship of pearl!
        And every chambered cell,
Where its dim dreaming life was wont to dwell,
As the frail tenant shaped his growing shell,
        Before thee lies revealed,—
Its irised ceiling rent, its sunless crypt unsealed!

Year after year beheld the silent toil
        That spread his lustrous coil;
        Still, as the spiral grew,
He left the past year's dwelling for the new,
Stole with soft step its shining archway through,
        Built up its idle door,
Stretched in his last-found home,
        and knew the old no more.

Thanks for the heavenly message brought by thee,
        Child of the wandering sea,
        Cast from her lap, forlorn!
From thy dead lips a clearer note is born
Than ever Triton blew from wreathed horn!
        While on mine ear it rings,
Through the deep caves of thought
        I hear a voice that sings:

Build thee more stately mansions, O my soul,
        As the swift seasons roll!
        Leave thy low-vaulted past!
Let each new temple, nobler than the last,
Shut thee from heaven with a dome more vast,
        Till thou at length art free,
Leaving thine outgrown shell
        by life's unresting sea!

Sunset and evening star,
      And one clear call for me,
And may there be no moaning of the bar,
      When I put out to sea.

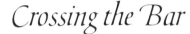
Crossing the Bar
Alfred, Lord Tennyson

But such a tide as moving seems asleep,
      Too full for sound and foam,
When that which drew from out the boundless deep
      Turns again home.

Twilight and evening bell,
      And after that the dark!
And may there be no sadness of farewell,
      When I embark;

For tho' from out our bourne of time and place
      The flood may bear me far,
I hope to see my Pilot face to face
      When I have crossed the bar.

Claude Monet: *The Beach at Sainte Adresse*, 1867.
Mr. and Mrs. Lewis L. Coburn Memorial Collection, courtesy of The Art Institute of Chicago.

Shall I Compare Thee to a Summer's Day?

William Shakespeare

Shall I compare thee to a summer's day?
Thou art more lovely and more temperate.
Rough winds do shake the darling buds of May,
And summer's lease hath all too short a date:
Sometime too hot the eye of heaven shines,
And often is his gold complexion dimm'd;
And every fair from fair some time declines,
By chance, or nature's changing course, untrimm'd;
But thy eternal summer shall not fade
Nor lose possession of that fair thou ow'st;
Nor shall Death brag thou wand'rest in his shade,
When in eternal lines to time thou grow'st.
    So long as men can breathe or eyes can see,
    So long lives this, and this gives life to thee.

Auguste Renoir: *Le Chapeau Epingle et la Baigneuse*.
Courtesy of The Art Institute of Chicago.

Auguste Renoir: *Near The Lake*, 1880.
Potter Palmer Collection, courtesy of The Art Institute of Chicago.

When I Was In Love With You

A. E. Housman

Oh, when I was in love with you,
  Then I was clean and brave,
And miles around the wonder grew
  How well did I behave.

And now the fancy passes by,
  And nothing will remain,
And miles around they'll say that I
  Am quite myself again.

Henri Matisse: From *Poesies de Mallarme: Doric Column.*
A. Peter Dewey Memorial Gift, courtesy of The Art Institute of Chicago.

The Builders

Henry Wadsworth Longfellow

All are architects of Fate,
    Working in these walls of Time;
Some with massive deeds and great,
    Some with ornaments of rhyme.

Nothing useless is, or low;
    Each thing in its place is best;
And what seems but idle show
    Strengthens and supports the rest.

For the structure that we raise,
    Time is with materials filled;
Our todays and yesterdays
    Are the blocks with which we build.

Truly shape and fashion these;
    Leave no yawning gaps between;
Think not, because no man sees,
    Such things will remain unseen.

In the elder days of Art,
    Builders wrought with greatest care
Each minute and unseen part;
    For the gods see everywhere.

Let us do our work as well.
    Both the unseen and the seen;
Make the house where gods may dwell
    Beautiful, entire, and clean.

Else our lives are incomplete,
    Standing in these walls of Time,
Broken stairways, where the feet
    Stumble, as they seek to climb.

Build today, then, strong and sure,
    With a firm and ample base;
And ascending and secure
    Shall tomorrow find its place.

Thus alone can we attain
    To those turrets, where the eye
Sees the world as one vast plain,
    And one boundless reach of sky.

If

Rudyard Kipling

If you can keep your head when all about you
    Are losing theirs and blaming it on you;
If you can trust yourself when all men doubt you,
    But make allowance for their doubting too:
If you can wait and not be tired by waiting,
    Or, being lied about, don't deal in lies,
Or being hated don't give way to hating,
    And yet don't look too good, nor talk too wise;

If you can dream—and not make dreams your master;
    If you can think—
    and not make thoughts your aim,
If you can meet with Triumph and Disaster
    And treat those two impostors just the same:
If you can bear to hear the truth you've spoken
    Twisted by knaves to make a trap for fools,
Or watch the things you gave your life to, broken,
    And stoop and build 'em up with worn-out tools;

If you can make one heap of all your winnings
    And risk it on one turn of pitch-and-toss,
And lose, and start again at your beginnings,
    And never breathe a word about your loss:
If you can force your heart and nerve and sinew
    To serve your turn long after they are gone,
And so hold on when there is nothing in you
    Except the Will which says to them: "Hold on!"

If you can talk with crowds and keep your virtue,
    Or walk with Kings—
    nor lose the common touch,
If neither foes nor loving friends can hurt you,
    If all men count with you, but none too much:
If you can fill the unforgiving minute
    With sixty seconds' worth of distance run,
Yours is the Earth and everything that's in it,
    And—which is more—you'll be a Man, my son!

Camille Pissarro: *On The Banks Of The Marne, Winter,* 1886.
Mr. and Mrs. Lewis L. Coburn Memorial Collection, courtesy of The Art Institute of Chicago.

Ulysses

Alfred, Lord Tennyson

It little profits that an idle king,
By this still hearth, among these barren crags,
Matched with an aged wife, I mete and dole
Unequal laws unto a savage race,
That hoard, and sleep, and feed, and know not me.
I cannot rest from travel; I will drink
Life to the lees. All times I have enjoyed
Greatly, have suffered greatly, both with those
That loved me, and alone; on shore, and when
Through scudding drifts the rainy Hyades
Vexed the dim sea. I am become a name;
For always roaming with a hungry heart
Much have I seen and known—cities of men
And manners, climates, councils, governments,
Myself not least, but honored of them all—
And drunk delight of battle with my peers,
Far on the ringing plains of windy Troy.
I am a part of all that I have met;
Yet all experience is an arch wherethrough
Gleams that untraveled world whose margin fades
Forever and forever when I move.
How dull it is to pause, to make an end,
To rust unburnished, not to shine in use!
As though to breathe were life! Life piled on life
Were all too little, and of one to me
Little remains; but every hour is saved
From that eternal silence, something more,
A bringer of new things; and vile it were
For some three suns to store and hoard myself,
And this gray spirit yearning in desire
To follow knowledge like a sinking star,
Beyond the utmost bound of human thought.
    This is my son, mine own Telemachus,
To whom I leave the scepter and the isle—
Well-loved of me, discerning to fulfill
This labor, by slow prudence to make mild
A rugged people, and through soft degrees
Subdue them to the useful and the good.
Most blameless is he, centered in the sphere
Of common duties, decent not to fail
In offices of tenderness, and pay
Meet adoration to my household gods,
When I am gone. He works his work, I mine.
    There lies the port; the vessel puffs her sail;
There gloom the dark, broad seas. My mariners,
Souls that have toiled, and wrought,
                    and thought with me—

Auguste Renoir: *Louis Valtat*, 1904.
Gift of Walter S. Brewster, courtesy of The Art Institute of Chicago.

That ever with a frolic welcome took
The thunder and the sunshine, and opposed
Free hearts, free foreheads—you and I are old;
Old age hath yet his honor and his toil.
Death closes all; but something ere the end,
Some work of noble note, may yet be done,
Not unbecoming men that strove with gods.
The lights begin to twinkle from the rocks;
The long day wanes; the slow moon climbs; the deep
Moans round with many voices. Come, my friends.
'Tis not too late to seek a newer world.
Push off, and sitting well in order smite
The sounding furrows; for my purpose holds
To sail beyond the sunset, and the baths
Of all the western stars, until I die.
It may be that the gulfs will wash us down;
It may be we shall touch the Happy Isles,
And see the great Achilles, whom we knew.
Though much is taken much abides; and though
We are not now that strength which in old days
Moved earth and heaven, that which we are, we are—
One equal temper of heroic hearts,
Made weak by time and fate, but strong in will
To strive, to seek, to find, and not to yield.

The Lamb

William Blake

Little Lamb, who made thee?
Dost thou know who made thee?
Gave thee life, and bid thee feed
By the stream and o'er the mead;
Gave thee clothing of delight,
Softest clothing, woolly, bright;
Gave thee such a tender voice,
Making all the vales rejoice?
Little Lamb, who made thee?
Dost thou know who made thee?

Little Lamb, I'll tell thee,
Little Lamb, I'll tell thee:
He is called by thy name,
For He calls Himself a Lamb.
He is meek, and He is mild;
He became a little child.
I a child, and thou a lamb,
We are called by His name.
Little Lamb, God bless thee!
Little Lamb, God bless thee!

Auguste Renoir: *Girl With A Hoop*, 1885.
Chester Dale Collection, National Gallery of Art, Washington, D.C.

Barbara Allen

Anonymous

In Scarlet town, where I was born,
There was a fair maid dwellin',
Made every youth cry Well-a-way!
Her name was Barbara Allen.

All in the merry month of May,
When green buds they were swellin',
Young Jemmy Grove on his death-bed lay,
For love of Barbara Allen.

He sent his man in to her then,
To the town where she was dwellin',
"O haste and come to my master dear,
If your name be Barbara Allen."

So slowly, slowly rase she up,
And slowly she came nigh him,
And when she drew the curtain by—
"Young man, I think you're dyin'."

Henri Matisse: Etching from *Poesies de Stephane Mallarme,* 1932.
A. Peter Dewey Memorial Gift, courtesy of The Art Institute of Chicago.

70

"O it's I am sick and very very sick,
And it's all for Barbara Allen."
"O the better for me ye'se never be,
Though your heart's blood were a-spillin'!"

"O dinna ye mind, young man," says she,
"When the red wine ye were fillin',
That ye made the healths go round and round,
And slighted Barbara Allen?"

He turned his face unto the wall,
And death was with him dealin':
"Adieu, adieu, my dear friends all,
And be kind to Barbara Allen!"

As she was walking o'er the fields,
She heard the dead-bell knellin';
And every jow the dead-bell gave
Cried "Woe to Barbara Allen."

"O mother, mother, make my bed,
O make it saft and narrow:
My love has died for me to-day,
I'll die for him to-morrow."

"Farewell," she said, "ye virgins all,
And shun the fault I fell in:
Henceforth take warning by the fall
Of cruel Barbara Allen."

Claude Monet: *Bordighera*, 1884.
Potter Palmer Collection, courtesy of The Art Institute of Chicago.

A Song From Sylvan

Louise Imogen Guiney

The little cares that fretted me,
I lost them yesterday
Among the fields above the sea,
Among the winds at play;
Among the lowing herds,
The rustling of the trees,
Among the singing birds,
The humming of the bees.

The fears of what may come to pass,
I cast them all away,
Among the clover-scented grass,
Among the new-mown hay;
Among the husking of the corn,
Where the drowsy poppies nod,
Where ill thoughts die and good are born,
Out in the fields with God.

Annabel Lee

Edgar Allen Poe

It was many and many a year ago,
   In a kingdom by the sea,
That a maiden there lived whom you may know
   By the name of Annabel Lee;—
And this maiden she lived with no other thought
   Than to love and be loved by me.

I was a child and she was a child,
   In this kingdom by the sea,
But we loved with a love that was more than love—
   I and my Annabel Lee—
With a love that the winged seraphs in Heaven
   Coveted her and me.

And this was the reason that, long ago,
   In this kingdom by the sea,
A wind blew out of a cloud, chilling
   My beautiful Annabel Lee;
So that her high-born kinsmen came
   And bore her away from me,
To shut her up in a sepulcher
   In this kingdom by the sea.

The angels, not half so happy in Heaven,
    Went envying her and me:—
Yes!—that was the reason (as all men know,
    In this kingdom by the sea)
That the wind came out of the cloud, by night,
    Chilling and killing my Annabel Lee.

But our love it was stronger by far than the love
    Of those who were older than we—
    Of many far wiser than we—
And neither the angels in Heaven above,
    Nor the demons down under the sea,
Can ever dissever my soul from the soul
    Of the beautiful Annabel Lee:—

For the moon never beams
    without bringing me dreams
    Of the beautiful Annabel Lee;
And the stars never rise but I feel the bright eyes
    Of the beautiful Annabel Lee;
And so, all the night-tide, I lie down by the side
Of my darling, my darling,—my life and my bride,
    In her sepulcher there by the sea—
    In her tomb by the sounding sea.

Pablo Picasso: *Visage.*
Gift of Walter S. Brewster, courtesy of The Art Institute of Chicago.

Should auld acquaintance be forgot,
And never brought to min'?
Should auld acquaintance be forgot,
And auld lang syne?

Auld Lang Syne

Robert Burns

(Chorus)
For auld lang syne, my dear,
For auld lang syne,
We'll tak a cup o' kindness yet
For auld lang syne.

And surely ye'll be your pint-stowp,
And surely I'll be mine!
And we'll tak a cup o' kindness yet
For auld lang syne.

We twa hae run about the braes,
And pu'd the gowans fine;
But we've wandered monie a weary fit
Sin' auld lang syne.

We twa hae paidled i' the burn,
From mornin' sun till dine;
But seas between us braid hae roared
Sin' auld lang syne.

And there's a hand, my trusty fiere,
And gie's a hand o' thine;
And we'll tak a right guid-willie waught
For auld lang syne.

Auguste Renoir: *The Rower's Lunch*, 1879/80.
Potter Palmer Collection, courtesy of The Art Institute of Chicago.

Set in Shakespeare roman, designed by
Gudrun Zapf von Hesse exclusively for Hallmark Editions.
Printed on Hallmark Crown Royale Book paper.
Designed by William M. Gilmore.